DAVID WENTZ

John Wesley's Give Me Your Hand

*Set in Modern Language with Introduction and
Suggestions for Group Use*

DOING CHRISTIANITY
Pastor David Wentz

First edition

ISBN: 979-8-9906172-6-1

This book was professionally typeset on Reedsy. Find out more at reedsy.com

"By this everyone will know that you are my disciples, if you have love for one another."

— JOHN 13:35

Contents

Introduction

By David Wentz

"Real Christians vote for A! If you support B you're [*insert worst insult you can think of*], and I'll never talk to you again!"

Has anyone ever said this to you?

Have you said it yourself, or posted it on social media?

I know I've read it often enough.

The interesting thing is, if the person doesn't specify who they're talking about, I often can't tell at first. Many times, supporters of A and supporters of B say exactly the same thing about each other.

There are good, sincere, educated Christians on both sides of the current political divide in America. Many are pastors and other colleagues I've worked with for decades. Some I agree with, and some I believe are misguided. But despite our often strong differences of opinion, I expect to see them all in heaven.

Some would say I'm deceiving myself if I think I can be friends with someone who doesn't share my opinions. They'd call me a hypocrite, or accuse me of being wishy-washy or afraid to stand up for the truth.

John Wesley, the founder of Methodism and grandfather of Pentacostalism, the Holiness movement, and the Salvation Army, was no stranger to people attacking him for his ideas. What would he say about how Christians should relate to those with different opinions?

We don't have to wonder. In 1750 he published a sermon on the topic. We'll go through that sermon in depth in this study. And if, at the end, we don't agree with each other, I hope we all will still be able to say, "Give me your hand."

Which Denomination Is Right?

In the England of Wesley's day, the division was not about politics. The flashpoint in that culture was disagreements over religion. Almost everyone considered themselves Christian. The issue was which particular denominational beliefs and practices best represented true Biblical Christianity.

In earlier centuries, Great Britain had seen bloody civil wars fought largely over these questions, especially between Protestants and Roman Catholics. By Wesley's time, the monarchy was firmly in Protestant hands.

By far the largest denomination was the state-sponsored Church of England, or Anglican Church. This was the "established" church, the church to belong to if you valued political and social approval. Wesley himself was a priest of the Anglican Church, and remained one all his life. But other Christian groups were also allowed: Puritans, Anabaptists, Presbyterians, Quakers, and more. And, of course, there was still a large minority of Roman Catholics, though most of the Protestant groups had serious doubts about whether Roman Catholics were true Christians — and vice versa. A sprinkling of Jews, mystics, and atheists rounded out the religious picture.

John Wesley never wanted to start a new denomination. His goal was to reform the Church of England. For a hundred years it had been the official state religion, and in many ways it had settled into bureaucratic institutional complacency. Many of the priests and church leaders who were comfortable with this found Wesley's calls for reform threatening.

They lashed back by attacking all Methodists as dangerous fanatics. Many Methodists, in return, thought all Anglicans were heathens who needed to be saved and born again. Both groups thought all the other denominations were off base. And many people in all groups thought it their Christian duty to shun each other. "If you support denomination A I'll be your friend, but if you say anything good about denomination B, go away and don't come back!"

That cultural division was the setting for the sermon in this book.

It's a sad fact of human nature that religious differences can cause the bitterest divisions and most passionate denouncements. People disagree about things all the time, and still get along. As someone said, "If two people agree on everything, one of them is unnecessary!" But add religion to the mix, and things take on a whole different flavor. That's because religion is not just about preferences, it's about ultimate truth and eternal destiny. If a person admits they might be wrong about religion, what does that mean for their hope to go to heaven?

Words Change

When I was in high school, something good was "groovy" or "far out." To my grandchildren, something good is "sick" (at the time of this writing!) Fifty years ago, I could go to jail for swiping a credit card, because back then, "swipe" meant "steal." Today, swiping a card means sliding it through the machine at the checkout counter.

If words can change meaning so radically in just fifty years, think how much they can change in three hundred![1]

A perfect example is the title of this sermon. A few years ago, I wanted to give our youth pastor a chance to preach. He asked me for a sermon idea. I told him to read this sermon and put it in his own words. He thought I was kidding, because when John Wesley wrote this sermon in 1750, he titled it, "Catholic Spirit." Why would I want my youth pastor to preach a Catholic sermon in a Methodist church?

As you've guessed by now, "catholic" is one of those words that meant something very different two hundred years ago than it does today. Today "catholic" is a noun, almost always capitalized and used exclusively to refer to the Roman Catholic denomination. In Wesley's day, "catholic" was an adjective.

The traditional English translation of the Apostles' Creed uses it that way when it says, "I believe in the holy catholic church." Many printed versions have an asterisk after the word "catholic," with a footnote saying, "universal." Asterisk or not, probably every Protestant pastor who uses the creed has had to explain that they are not asking their people to proclaim allegiance to the Pope.

Do you wonder why I didn't use *John Wesley's "Catholic Spirit"* as the title of this book?

No one modern word adequately conveys the eighteenth-century range of meanings of "catholic." As is so often the case, the context determines the exact sense.

- In the creed, as the footnote indicates, it means "universal," the universal church being all Christians of every time, place, and denominational or non-denominational affiliation.

- When referring to food or music, "a catholic taste" can mean enjoyment of an eclectic or wide-ranging variety.
- In discussing attitudes toward religious beliefs, as in Wesley's sermon, the meaning is some combination of "tolerant," " inclusive," "ecumenical," "broad-minded," and "open" or "open-minded."

In this paraphrase, I have usually chosen "open." I believe that best conveys the shade of meaning Wesley has in mind here.

Wesley certainly encourages open-mindedness with respect to religion, but only within the clearly defined boundaries of historic Christian belief. As we'll see, he sets clear limits. Wesley would probably agree with the wit who said, "Some people are so open-minded their brains fall out."

Who in the World Are Jehu and Jehonadab?

Wesley's text, or theme verse, for this sermon is 2 Kings 10:15, rendered here in the New King James translation (NKJV):

> *Now when he departed from there, he [Jehu] met Jehonadab the son of Rechab, coming to meet him; and he greeted him and said to him, "Is your heart right, as my heart is toward your heart?" And Jehonadab answered, "It is." Jehu said, "If it is, give me your hand."*

Who in the world are Jehu and Jehonadab?

After King Solomon died, his son Rehoboam became king. The ten northern tribes of the Hebrews rebelled against Rehoboam and formed the Kingdom of Israel. The two southern tribes stuck with Rehoboam and became the Kingdom of Judah. Jehu was a later king of the northern kingdom. His story is fascinating (you can read it in 2 Kings 9 and 10), but Wesley's only concern with Jehu in this sermon is the question he asked of Jehonadab.

Jehonadab (also spelled Jonadab) was the head of a tribe of nomads, probably sheep-herders, who were related to Moses by marriage. They lived in the land of Israel beside the Hebrews. Jehonadab founded a group called the Rechabites (named after his father Rechab), who lived in tents and did not drink wine or plant crops.[2] Again, it's a fascinating story, but Wesley's only concern here is his conversation with Jehu, quoted in the text verse.

Notes on the Paraphrase

John Wesley's teachings and writings were clear, logical, and Biblical. They sparked a revival that could not be contained in the established church, and its effects are still felt today.

Wesley's logic, clarity, and Biblical truth are as potent as they ever were. Unfortunately, his three-hundred-year-old English is more and more difficult for modern readers to understand. Wesley was a revival preacher with the best of them. People were often so struck by his words that they cried out and even fell to the ground. Today, the mental effort of interpreting his archaic phrases can rob them of their power.

That's where this book comes in. I've put Wesley's words into modern English, while as much as possible maintaining his original structure and style. My goal is not only to help you understand Wesley's points but to give you a sense of what it was like to hear him preach.

I believe Wesley would approve. He wrote, "I design plain truth for plain people... I labor to avoid all words which are not easy to be understood, all which are not used in common life."[4]

Besides being a powerful revival preacher, Wesley had a genius for organizing those who responded to his messages so they could keep growing in faith and living in holiness. As his movement grew, Wesley gathered fifty-eight of his most important sermons into a book which he published for his lay preachers to read, learn, and then preach in their own words. "Give Me Your Hand," under it's original title of "Catholic Spirit," is number thirty-nine of the fifty-eight. While you can read it straight through, as Wesley's original listeners would have heard it, I've broken it up here into bite-size sections to make it easier to discuss and digest. For scholars and the curious, Wesley's original is included as Appendix 2.

John Wesley's brother, Charles, wrote over 3,000 hymns in his lifetime. Many of them put the essence of John's teaching to rhyme and music. His hymn, "Catholic Love," is a great example. It was added at the end of this sermon in some of the early printed editions. You can find it in Appendix 1. The words can be sung to the same tune as "Faith of Our Fathers."

Though one of the most widely read men of his time, John Wesley called himself "a man of one book."[5] That book was the Bible. His sermons are liberally sprinkled with Scripture quotations and allusions.

Wesley read the Bible in Greek, Hebrew, and probably German, but for him the English Bible was the King James Version, translated in 1611. For many modern readers, that seventeenth-century English can be even more difficult than Wesley's eighteenth-century phrasing. For Bible references in this paraphrase, I chose either the New Revised Standard

Version (NRSV) or the New King James Version (NKJV). Both are clear, accurate translations that trace their literary lineage back to the King James Version used by Wesley. The NRSV is more widely used in Methodist churches, so that was my default translation. In some cases where the NKJV more closely reflected Wesley's wording, I used that translation and noted it. This is particularly the case with the text verse.

For clarity, verses and phrases that are direct quotes from the Bible are placed in italics. The many places where Wesley alluded to Scripture without specifically quoting it are in regular print. All quotes and allusions I could identify are footnoted.

Finally, the methodical Wesley commonly used the technique of numbering his paragraphs. I have replaced the numbers with subheadings and divided his long block paragraphs into shorter ones to reflect modern usage.

Suggestions for Group Use

John Wesley wrote "Give Me Your Hand" as a sermon, and this version can certainly be read straight through in that way. However, as with all thought-provoking books, Wesley's words will have the greatest impact on our individual lives and on our churches when we discuss them with others.

That was John Wesley's philosophy. Wesley organized his followers into small groups called "classes" which met weekly, usually in people's homes. Their main purpose was to discuss how they could be better Christians, based on the previous week's sermon, and to hold each other accountable for acting that way. Of course, as part of that they experienced a wonderful, joyful fellowship. In the modern phrase, they were "doing life together."

This book is perfectly suited for that kind of small-group experience. It can be a home group, a coffee shop gathering, or an adult Sunday School class. To facilitate such use, I have broken the material into six parts. Each should take less than twenty minutes to read. I have also included discussion questions at the end of each part, to get you started. (If you are reading this book on your own, don't skip the questions. Ask God to give you more wisdom as you prayerfully think about them, not just as you read but in quiet moments throughout the day.)

How to Lead a Small Group

Small group gatherings are easy. You can meet in the same place every time, or in different people's homes. You can have the same leader every time, or rotate leadership. (Being the leader isn't a big deal. The leader is just the person who reads the discussion questions out loud.) A good time frame is an hour to an hour and a half. The tried and true format goes something like this:

- People arrive, say hello, and perhaps munch on some light refreshments.
- Somebody says a prayer to get things started, asking God to guide the conversation and bless anyone who is missing.
- You catch up on anything left over from your last meeting – especially any good stories about how the study helped someone during the week.
- You talk about as many of the discussion questions as you have time for. Answer the ones that interest you, or make

up your own.
- You set the place, time, and assignments for the next meeting.
- You share prayer concerns and pray for them.
- You go out and live what you've been talking about.

If anyone was absent, the leader or a designated person should call them within a day. Tell them you missed them, see if anything is wrong, and catch them up on what happened. Don't forget to tell them the details of the next meeting.

Suggested Schedule

Six weeks is a good, non-threatening length of time for most people to commit to a study like this. Here's a suggested schedule.

Week 1: Introduction
Week 2: Why Is It So Hard to Love One Another?
Week 3: Differences Are Not Deal Breakers
Week 4: The Questions That Matter
Week 5: Give Me Your Hand
Week 6: True Openness

* * *

Discussion Questions

(1) What is your religious background?

- Raised in a church of this denomination (if you are studying with a church group)
- Raised in a church of another denomination(s) or no denomination
- Raised in church but been away for a while
- Not raised in church

(2) What do you hope to get out of this study?

(3) Without getting into a political discussion (please!), with respect to the opening quotes about how "real" Christians vote:

- Do you know people who feel this way?
- Do you sometimes feel this way?
- How do you relate to people on "the other side?"

(4) If you are studying this in a church group, why did you initially choose to attend this church?

- How important were this church's doctrinal beliefs in your choice?
- How important were this church's worship practices in your choice?

(6) What do you think of the saying, "Some people are so open-minded that their brains fall out?"

* * *

Notes

[1] That's why there are so many modern translations of the Bible. Most people just don't understand the King James Version, written over four hundred years ago in 1611.

[2] *But they answered, "We will drink no wine, for our ancestor Jonadab son of Rechab commanded us, 'You shall never drink wine, neither you nor your children; nor shall you ever build a house, or sow seed; nor shall you plant a vineyard, or even own one; but you shall live in tents all your days, that you may live many days in the land where you reside.'"* (Jeremiah 35:6–7)

[3] Portions of the remaining part of the introduction duplicate similar parts in other books in the John Wesley in Modern Language series.

[4] "Preface to the Sermons," from *The Works of John Wesley*, Third American Edition, 1872. Language updated.

[5] *The Works of John Wesley*, Third American Edition, 1872. 7:203

1

Why Is It So Hard to Love One Another?

Now when he departed from there, he met Jehonadab the son of Rechab, coming to meet him; and he greeted him and said to him, "Is your heart right, as my heart is toward your heart?" And Jehonadab answered, "It is." Jehu said, "If it is, give me your hand." — 2 Kings 10:15 NKJV

Everyone admits, even those who don't actually do it, that we owe love to every human being. The royal law, *You shall love your neighbor as yourself,*[1] is self-explanatory. It doesn't mean the miserable understanding the ancient legalists put on it, "You shall love your neighbor" — who they defined as your relatives and friends and acquaintances — "and hate your enemy."[2] No indeed.

But I say to you, said our Lord, *Love your enemies and pray for those who persecute you, so that you may be children,* in a way that everyone can see, *of your Father in heaven; for he makes his sun rise on the evil and on the good, and sends rain on the righteous and on the unrighteous.*[3]

But there certainly is a particular kind of love which we owe to those who love God. King David said all his delight was in the saints who are on the earth, and in those who excel in virtue.[4]

In the same way, one greater than David said, *I give you a new commandment, that you love one another. Just as I have loved you, you also should love one another. By this everyone will know that you are my disciples, if you have love for one another.*[5]

This is the love the Apostle John so frequently and strongly insists on:

- *This,* he said, *is the message you have heard from the beginning, that we should love one another.*[6]
- *We know love by this, that he laid down his life for us—and we ought,* if love calls us to this point, *to lay down our lives for one another.*[7]
- And again, *Beloved, let us love one another, because love is from God; everyone who loves is born of God and knows God. Whoever does not love does not know God, for God is love.*[8]
- *In this is love, not that we loved God but that he loved us and sent his Son to be the atoning sacrifice for our sins. Beloved, since God loved us so much, we also ought to love one another.*[9]

Everyone agrees with this; but does everyone practice it? Daily experience shows the opposite. Where are even the Christians who love one another as he has commanded us to? So many hindrances lie in the way!

Two Great Hindrances

The two great, general hindrances to Christians loving each other are, first, that they can't all think the same way, and second, because of this, they can't all do things the same way. In many small issues, the way they do things has to differ, because what they believe about those things differs.

So, a difference in theological opinions or particular worship practices may prevent Christians with different understandings and approaches from uniting in the same denomination. Does that have to prevent us from uniting in affection for each other? Though we cannot think the same way, may we not love the same way? May we not be of one heart, though we are not of one opinion?

Without any doubt, we may. All the children of God may unite in this way, regardless of these smaller distinctions. Even with our differences, we may still encourage one another in love and good deeds.[10]

Surely, in this respect, the example of Jehu himself, as mixed a character as he was, is well worthy of both the attention and imitation of every serious Christian.

Now when he departed from there, he met Jehonadab the son of Rechab, coming to meet him; and he greeted him and said to him, "Is your heart right, as my heart is toward your heart?" And Jehonadab answered, "It is." Jehu said, "If it is, give me your hand."

This verse, our sermon text, naturally divides itself into two parts:

First, a question Jehu asks Jehonadab: *"Is your heart right, as my heart is toward your heart?"*

Second, Jehu's offer, after Jehonadab answers that it is: *"If it is, give me your hand."*

* * *

Discussion Questions

(1) What is the difference between *You shall love your neighbor as yourself*, and *Just as I have loved you, you also should love one another?*

- What kinds of differences in behavior or relationships might this imply?

(2) In one denomination, pastors are hired and fired by the local congregation. In another, pastors are appointed by a bishop.

- Can those two denominations unite into one without one group or the other changing their beliefs and practices?
- Can those two denominations demonstrate Christian unity in other ways without one or the other changing their beliefs and practices?

(3) Is it necessary for one denomination to be wrong in order for another to be right?

(4) What Christian beliefs or practices do you consider essential, so that if you had to give them up you wouldn't feel like you were properly living your faith?

- What makes them essential?
- Are they worth fighting for?
- If so, what should that fight look like?

(5) How do you think God defines Christian unity?

* * *

Notes

[1] *Honor your father and mother; also, You shall love your neighbor as yourself.* (Matthew 19:19)

[2] *You have heard that it was said, "You shall love your neighbor and hate your enemy.'* (Matthew 5:43)

[3] *But I say to you, Love your enemies and pray for those who persecute you, so that you may be children of your Father in heaven; for he makes his sun rise on the evil and on the good, and sends rain on the righteous and on the unrighteous.* (Matthew 5:44–45)

[4] *As for the holy ones in the land, they are the noble, in whom is all my delight.* (Psalm 16:3)

[5] *I give you a new commandment, that you love one another. Just as I have loved you, you also should love one another. By this everyone will know that you are my disciples, if you have love for one another."* (John 13:34–35)

[6] *For this is the message you have heard from the beginning, that we should love one another.* (1 John 3:11)

[7] *We know love by this, that he laid down his life for us—and we ought to lay down our lives for one another.* (1 John 3:16)

[8] *Beloved, let us love one another, because love is from God; everyone who loves is born of God and knows God. Whoever does not love does not know God, for God is love.* (1 John 4:7–8)

[9] *In this is love, not that we loved God but that he loved us and sent his Son to be the atoning sacrifice for our sins. Beloved, since God loved us so much, we also ought to love one another.* (1 John

4:10–11)

¹⁰ *And let us consider how to provoke one another to love and good deeds.* (Hebrews 10:24)

2

Differences Are Not Deal Breakers

Now when he departed from there, he met Jehonadab the son of Rechab, coming to meet him; and he greeted him and said to him, "Is your heart right, as my heart is toward your heart?" And Jehonadab answered, "It is." Jehu said, "If it is, give me your hand." — 2 Kings 10:15 NKJV

First, let's consider the question Jehu asks Jehonadab: *"Is your heart right, as my heart is toward your heart?"*

The first thing we can see in these words is that Jehu doesn't ask anything at all about Jehonadab's opinions. And yet he certainly held some which were very uncommon, indeed quite peculiar to himself, and they had a strong influence on the way he lived. In fact, he laid so great a stress on some of these as to require his children and all his descendents to live by them. This is evident from the account given by Jeremiah many years after Jehonadab's death.

I took Jaazaniah... and his brothers, and all his sons,

and the whole house of the Rechabites... I set before the Rechabites pitchers full of wine, and cups; and I said to them, "Have some wine." But they answered, "We will drink no wine, for our ancestor Jonadab son of Rechab commanded us, 'You shall never drink wine, neither you nor your children; nor shall you ever build a house, or sow seed; nor shall you plant a vineyard, or even own one; but you shall live in tents all your days'... We have obeyed and done all that our ancestor Jonadab commanded us."[1]

It's Alright to Have Different Religious Opinions

Jehu doesn't concern himself at all with any of these things (though it seems to have been Jehu's manner in things both secular and religious to drive *like a maniac*).[2] Instead, he lets Jehonadab think what he wants to. Neither of them appears to have given the other the slightest trouble about the opinions they maintained.

It's entirely possible that even these days many good people may entertain peculiar opinions. Some people may even be as strange about this as Jehonadab was. Certainly, as long as we *know only in part,*[3] everyone will not see everything the same way. It is an unavoidable consequence of the weakness and limitations of human understanding, that different people will be of different minds about religion, just as they are about the rest of life. So it has been from the beginning of the world, and so it will be *until the time of universal restoration.*[4]

To carry it further: everyone necessarily believes that every particular opinion they have is true — because to believe an opinion is not true is the same thing as not to have it. But no one can be assured that all of their opinions, taken together, are true. Indeed, every thinking person is sure that they are not, because, as the ancient saying goes, "To be ignorant of many things, and mistaken in some, is the necessary condition of humanity."[5] All thinking people know this is true in their own case. They know, in general, that they must be wrong in some opinions; they just don't know, and perhaps cannot know, which particular opinions are wrong.

I say, "perhaps cannot know," because who can tell how far invincible ignorance may extend? Or, what amounts to the same thing, invincible pre-judgment?[6] — which is often so deeply rooted in tender minds that it is impossible to later remove.

And who can say, without knowing every detail of a person's life, how far anyone can be judged guilty for holding any particular wrong opinion or pre-judgment? Because guilt requires some element of willfulness or conscious intention, and the only one who can judge that is God, *who searches the heart.*[7]

Every wise person, therefore, will allow others the same liberty of thinking that they want other people to allow them. I will no more insist on you embracing my opinions than I would want you to insist that I embrace yours. The wise person bears with those who differ. If there is someone with whom they desire to to be friends, they ask only one question: *"Is your heart right, as my heart is toward your heart?"*

It's Alright to Have Different Religious Practices

So first, we see that Jehu doesn't ask anything about Jehonadab's religious opinions. Second, we see that he asks nothing about Jehonadab's way of worship; although it is highly probable that there was, in this respect also, a very wide difference between them.

We have every reason to believe that Jehonadab, as well as all his descendants, worshipped God at Jerusalem. Jehu, on the other hand, did not. He was more interested in politics than religion. He did kill the worshippers of Baal and destroyed their religion out of Israel,[8] but he himself continued to worship the golden calves Jeroboam had set up,[9] because it was more convenient.[10]

But even among those of an upright heart, those who desire to always keep their conscience clear,[11] it must be that, as long as there are various religious opinions, there will be various ways of worshipping God. A variety of opinion necessarily implies a variety of practice. And as, throughout history, nothing has created bigger differences between people than their opinions concerning the Supreme Being, so nothing else has created bigger differences than the right way to worship him.

Had this been true only among non-Christians, it would not have been at all surprising. We know that they did not know God through their own wisdom,[12] so they could not know how to worship him. But isn't it strange that even in the Christian world, though we all agree in general that *God is spirit, and those who worship him must worship in spirit and truth,*[13] yet the particular ways of worshipping God are almost as various as among the heathens?

We Can't Force Others to Agree With Us

So how shall we choose among so much variety?

No one can choose for, or prescribe to, another. Every person must follow the dictates of their own conscience, in simplicity and godly sincerity. Every person must be fully persuaded in their own mind, and then act according to the best light they have.

In the same way, no one has the right to force someone else to live by their own rule. God has given no right to any of the children of humanity to lord it over the conscience of others in this way. Every person must judge for themselves, as every person must give an account of themselves to God.[14]

Every follower of Christ is obligated, by the very nature of Christianity, to be a member of some particular congregation or other; some church, as it is usually termed — which implies a particular way of worshipping God, for, *Can two walk together, unless they are agreed?*[15] Yet no one can be forced by any power on earth but that of their own conscience to prefer this or that congregation to another, this or that particular way of worship.

I know it is commonly supposed that the place of our birth fixes the denomination to which we ought to belong; that one, for instance, who is born in England ought to be a member of what is called the Church of England, and therefore should worship God in the particular manner which is prescribed by that Church. I once passionately defended this idea myself.

But now I find many reasons to lessen that passion. I now believe that idea carries with it such problems as no reasonable person can get over.

Not the least of those problems is this: if that rule had held firm, there could have been no Protestant Reformation. That rule entirely destroys the right of each person to make their own decisions. And that's what the whole Reformation stands on.

So I don't dare presume to impose my way of worship on anyone else. I believe it is truly ancient and apostolic, but my

23

belief is no rule for anyone else.

I don't ask someone with whom I would unite in Christian love, "Are you of my denomination? Do you accept the same form of church government, and the same church officers, with me? Do you use the same form of prayer that I use to worship God?"

I don't ask, "Do you receive the Lord's Supper the same way I do?" Nor, "In baptism, do you have the people answer the same questions we do, or agree with me about the proper age for baptism?" Indeed, as clear as I am in my own mind, I don't ask you if you even allow baptism and the Lord's Supper at all.

Let all these things go for now. We will talk of them, if need be, at a more convenient time. For now, my only question is this: *"Is your heart right, as my heart is toward your heart?"*

* * *

Discussion Questions

(1) Do you have a family rule or tradition that someone else might consider strange?

- If so, would you mind telling us?
- Where did it originate?
- Why do you continue to observe it?

(2) "It is an unavoidable consequence of the weakness and limitations of human understanding, that different people will be of different minds about religion, just as they are about the rest of life."

24

- Do you agree that this is the reason for different opinions?
- If people had more understanding, would they agree about more things?
- Is more education the key to more understanding? If not, what is?

(3) Wesley uses the terms "invincible ignorance" and "invincible pre-judgment."

- What do you think Wesley means by "invincible" in this context?
- Do you agree that some ignorance and pre-judgment is invincible?
- What do you do when you run across that in other people?
- Is it possible to identify it in yourself?

(4) "Every wise person, therefore, will allow others the same liberty of thinking that they want other people to allow them." Based on the context of this sermon:

- Is Wesley making an absolute statement that no one should ever try to change anyone else's mind?
- What situations is Wesley applying this to?

(5) "Isn't it strange that even in the Christian world, though we all agree in general that *God is spirit, and those who worship him must worship in spirit and truth,*[16] yet the particular ways of worshiping God are almost as various as among the heathens?"

- Why do you think God allows so many differences?
- Are there any ways people profess to worship God that are,

in fact, wrong?

- The Bible contains very little description of a Christian worship service. What does this say about the kind of worship God desires?

* * *

Notes

[1] Jeremiah 35:3–10.

Jeremiah spells the name "Jonadab" while the author of 1 Kings spells it "Jehonadab," but both are referring to the same person.

[2] *Again the sentinel reported, "He reached them, but he is not coming back. It looks like the driving of Jehu son of Nimshi; for he drives like a maniac."* (2 Kings 9:20) This comparison of Jehu's chariot-driving style with his approach to life in general is an example of John Wesley's dry humor.

[3] *For now we see in a mirror, dimly, but then we will see face to face. Now I know only in part; then I will know fully, even as I have been fully known.* (1 Corinthians 13:12)

[4] *Who must remain in heaven until the time of universal restoration that God announced long ago through his holy prophets.* (Acts 3:21)

[5] Wesley's rendering of a traditional ancient Greek proverb.

[6] Wesley's original word was "prejudice," but this is another word where the meaning has changed. He is not talking about bigotry toward people, but about forming a judgment concerning a matter before all the facts are known.

[7] *And God, who searches the heart, knows what is the mind of the Spirit, because the Spirit intercedes for the saints according to the will of God.* (Romans 8:27)

[8] This is described in detail in 2 Kings 10:18-27.

[9] When the ten northern tribes rebelled, Jeroboam became their first king. He set up golden calf idols in two northern cities so the people would not continue to go to Jerusalem (in the southern kingdom) to worship. See 1 Kings 6:26-29.

[10] *But Jehu did not turn aside from the sins of Jeroboam son of Nebat, which he caused Israel to commit—the golden calves that were in Bethel and in Dan.* (2 Kings 10:29)

Bethel was more convenient to Jehu's home base in the northern kingdom of Israel than traveling to the southern kingdom of Judea to worship in Jerusalem.

[11] *Therefore I do my best always to have a clear conscience toward God and all people.* (Acts 24:16)

[12] *For since, in the wisdom of God, the world did not know God through wisdom, God decided, through the foolishness of our proclamation, to save those who believe.* (1 Corinthians 1:21)

[13] John 4:24

[14] *And before him no creature is hidden, but all are naked and laid bare to the eyes of the one to whom we must render an account.* (Hebrews 4:13)

[15] Amos 3:3 NKJV

[16] John 4:24

3

The Questions That Matter

Now when he departed from there, he met Jehonadab the son of Rechab, coming to meet him; and he greeted him and said to him, "Is your heart right, as my heart is toward your heart?" And Jehonadab answered, "It is." Jehu said, "If it is, give me your hand." — 2 Kings 10:15 NKJV

What exactly does it mean to ask if a person's heart is right? I don't mean what was Jehu asking Jehonadab. What should a follower of Christ mean by that question when they ask it of someone else?

Here are the questions a Christian should ask of another before taking their hand.

Is Your Heart Right With God?

Do you believe God exists as perfect God?

- Do you believe in his eternity, his all-presence, his wisdom and power, his justice, mercy, and truth?

- Do you believe that he *sustains all things by his powerful word*,[1] and that he controls even the smallest, even the most unlovely things to his own glory and the good of those who love him?[2]
- Do you have a personal divine experience, a supernatural conviction, about the things of God?
- Do you *walk by faith, not by sight*,[3] looking not at things that will pass away, but things that are eternal?[4]

Do you believe in the Lord Jesus Christ, God over all, blessed forever?

- Do you have a personal revelation of him in your own soul?
- Do you know *Jesus Christ, and him crucified*?[5]
- Does he live in you, and you in him?[6]
- Is he formed in your heart by faith?[7]

Have you absolutely given up all claim to righteousness based on your own good works, and submitted yourself to the righteousness of God which is by faith in Christ Jesus?[8]

- Are you in Christ, not because of your own righteousness, but the righteousness which is by faith?[9]
- And are you, through Christ, fighting the good fight of faith, and laying hold of eternal life?[10]

Is your faith filled with the energy of love?

- Do you *love God* (I don't say "above all things," for that expression is both unscriptural and ambiguous, but) *with all your heart, and with all your soul, and with all your mind, and with all your strength?*[11]

- Do you seek all your happiness in him alone?
- And do you find what you seek?

Does your soul continually praise the Lord, and your spirit rejoice in God, your Savior?[12]

- Have you learned to give thanks in everything,[13] and do you find it a joyful and pleasant thing to be thankful?
- Is God the center of your soul, the sum of all your desires?
- Are you therefore storing up your treasures in heaven,[14] and counting everything else as sewage and waste?[15]
- Has the love of Christ cast the love of the world out of your soul?
- Then you are crucified to the world, you are dead to all here below, and *your life is hidden with Christ in God.*[16]

Are you busy doing, not your own will, but the will of God who sent you?[17]

— of him who sent you down to visit this world a while, to spend a few days in a foreign land,[18] until, having finished the work he gave you to do, you return to your Father's house?

Is it your meat and drink to do the will of your Father in heaven?□[19]

- Is your eye single-focused[20] in all things, always fixed on God, always looking to Jesus?
- Do you point at him in whatever you do, in all your labor,

your business, your conversation?
- Do you aim only at the glory of God in everything,[21] *in word or deed, doing everything in the name of the Lord Jesus, giving thanks to God the Father through him?*[22]

Does the love of God cause you to serve him with awe and rejoice in him with reverence?

- Are you more afraid of displeasing God than you are of death or hell?
- Is nothing as terrible to you as the thought of offending the eyes of God's glory?
- Based on this, do you hate all evil ways,[23] every transgression of God's holy and perfect law, and instead do your best to always have a clear conscience toward God and all people?"[24]

Is Your Heart Right With People?

Is your heart right toward your neighbors?

- Do you love every person, without exception, as you love yourself?[25] *If you love only those who love you, what credit is that to you?* [26]

Do you love your enemies?[27]

- Is your soul full of good will and tender affection toward them?
- Do you love even the enemies of God, the unthankful and unholy?

- Does your heart yearn over them?
- Could you wish yourself cursed by God in this life for their sake?[28]
- And do you show this by blessing those who curse you and praying for those who spitefully use you and persecute you?[29]

Do you show your love by your works?

- When you have time and opportunity, do you in fact do good to all people, neighbors or strangers, friends or enemies, good or bad?
- Do you do them all the good you can?
- Do you try to supply all their needs, assisting them both in body and soul, to the utmost of your ability?

"If this is your mindset," may every Christian say, "or if you sincerely desire it to be and you intend to work on it until you get there, then your heart is *right, as my heart is toward your heart.*"

* * *

Discussion Questions

(1) Wesley makes the questions in this section the conditions for determining if one's heart is right. How are these points different from what he calls matters of opinion in the previous section?

(2) Which of these questions do you think are most important? Why?

(3) Do you think any of these questions are not important to being a true Christian? Why?

(4) John Wesley described how he received a personal revelation of Jesus in his soul in these words from his journal entry for May 24, 1738:

> *"In the evening I went very unwillingly to a society in Aldersgate Street, where one was reading Luther's preface to the Epistle to the Romans. About a quarter before nine, while he was describing the change which God works in the heart through faith in Christ, I felt my heart strangely warmed.*
>
> *"I felt I did trust in Christ, Christ alone for salvation; and an assurance was given to me that he had taken away my sins, even mine, and saved me from the law of sin and death."*

- What is your own experience of a revelation of Jesus in your soul?

(5) How many people do you know who could answer yes to all the questions in this section?

(6) Which of these questions, if any, do you need to work on in your own life?

- How will you do that?

* * *

Notes

[1] *He is the reflection of God's glory and the exact imprint of God's very being, and he sustains all things by his powerful word. When he had made purification for sins, he sat down at the right hand of the Majesty on high.* (Hebrews 1:3)

[2] *We know that all things work together for good for those who love God, who are called according to his purpose.* (Romans 8:28)

[3] *For we walk by faith, not by sight.* (2 Corinthians 5:7)

[4] *Because we look not at what can be seen but at what cannot be seen; for what can be seen is temporary, but what cannot be seen is eternal.* (2 Corinthians 4:18)

[5] *For I decided to know nothing among you except Jesus Christ, and him crucified.* (1 Corinthians 2:2)

[6] *By this we know that we abide in him and he in us, because he has given us of his Spirit.* (1 John 4:13)

[7] *My little children, for whom I am again in the pain of childbirth until Christ is formed in you.* (Galatians 4:19)

[8] *For, being ignorant of the righteousness that comes from God, and seeking to establish their own, they have not submitted to God's righteousness.* (Romans 10:3)

[9] *And be found in him, not having a righteousness of my own that comes from the law, but one that comes through faith in Christ, the righteousness from God based on faith.* (Philippians 3:9)

[10] *Fight the good fight of the faith; take hold of the eternal life, to which you were called and for which you made the good confession in the presence of many witnesses.* (1 Timothy 6:12)

[11] *You shall love the Lord your God with all your heart, and with all your soul, and with all your mind, and with all your strength.* (Mark 12:30)

[12] *And Mary said, "My soul magnifies the Lord, and my spirit rejoices in God my Savior."* (Luke 1:46–47)

[13] *Giving thanks to God the Father at all times and for everything in the name of our Lord Jesus Christ.* (Ephesians 5:20)

[14] *But store up for yourselves treasures in heaven, where neither moth nor rust consumes and where thieves do not break in and steal.* (Matthew 6:20)

[15] *More than that, I regard everything as loss because of the surpassing value of knowing Christ Jesus my Lord. For his sake I have suffered the loss of all things, and I regard them as rubbish, in order that I may gain Christ.* (Philippians 3:8)

[16] *For you have died, and your life is hidden with Christ in God.* (Colossians 3:3)

[17] *For I have come down from heaven, not to do my own will, but the will of him who sent me.* (John 6:38)

[18] *She bore a son, and he named him Gershom; for he said, "I have been an alien residing in a foreign land."* (Exodus 2:22)

[19] *Not everyone who says to me, 'Lord, Lord,' will enter the kingdom of heaven, but only the one who does the will of my Father in heaven.* (Matthew 7:21)

[20] *The eye is the lamp of the body. So, if your eye is healthy, your whole body will be full of light.* (Matthew 6:22) Instead of "healthy," KJV reads "single."

[21] *In the same way, let your light shine before others, so that they may see your good works and give glory to your Father in heaven.* (Matthew 5:16)

[22] *And whatever you do, in word or deed, do everything in the name of the Lord Jesus, giving thanks to God the Father through him.*

(Colossians 3:17)

²³ *The fear of the Lord is hatred of evil. Pride and arrogance and the way of evil and perverted speech I hate.* (Proverbs 8:13)

²⁴ *Therefore I do my best always to have a clear conscience toward God and all people.* (Acts 24:16)

²⁵ *The second is this, "You shall love your neighbor as yourself." There is no other commandment greater than these.* (Mark 12:31)

²⁶ *If you love those who love you, what credit is that to you? For even sinners love those who love them.* (Luke 6:32)

²⁷ *But I say to you that listen, Love your enemies, do good to those who hate you.* (Luke 6:27)

²⁸ *For I could wish that I myself were accursed and cut off from Christ for the sake of my own people, my kindred according to the flesh.* (Romans 9:3)

²⁹ *But I say to you, love your enemies, bless those who curse you, do good to those who hate you, and pray for those who spitefully use you and persecute you.* (Matthew 5:44 NKJV)

4

Give Me Your Hand

Now when he departed from there, he met Jehonadab the son of Rechab, coming to meet him; and he greeted him and said to him, "Is your heart right, as my heart is toward your heart?" And Jehonadab answered, "It is." Jehu said, "If it is, give me your hand." — 2 Kings 10:15 NKJV

You Don't Have to Agree With Me

If it is, give me your hand.

I don't mean, "Be of my opinion." That's not necessary; I don't expect it or desire it.

Neither do I mean, "I will be of your opinion." I can't, I don't have that choice. I can no more choose what I think than I can choose what I see or hear. You keep your opinion, and I'll keep mine, just as strongly as ever. You don't even need to try to come over to me, or bring me over to you. I don't want you to argue with me about those points where we differ; I don't want to hear or speak one word about them. Leave all opinions alone, on either side. Just *give me your hand.*

You Don't Have to Do Things My Way

I don't mean, "Worship the way I do," or "I'll worship the way you do." This also is a thing which does not depend either on your choice or mine. We must both act as each is fully persuaded in our own mind. You hold on to what you believe is most acceptable to God, and I will do the same.

I believe the Church of England form of church government is scriptural and apostolic. If you think the Presbyterian or non-denominational is better, keep thinking that, and act accordingly.

I believe infants ought to be baptized, and that this may be done either by dipping or sprinkling. If you think differently, keep thinking that way, and follow the way you think is right.

It seems to me that written prayers read by everyone together are of excellent use, especially in church services. If you judge extemporaneous prayer to be of more use, act suitable to your own judgment.

My belief is that I ought not forbid it if someone wants to be baptized,[1] and that I ought to eat bread and drink wine in remembrance of my dying Master.[2] However, if you are not convinced of this, act according to the understanding you have.

I have no desire to argue with you one moment upon any of these topics. Put all these smaller points aside, and let them never come into sight. If your heart is as my heart, if you love God and all humankind, I ask no more: *give me your hand.*

Love Me

Here's what I do mean.

First, love me. Not just the way you love every person. Not just they way you love your enemies, or the enemies of God, those who hate you and are mean to you and persecute you.[3] Not just the way you love strangers you don't know anything about. I'm not satisfied with this. No, if your heart is *right, as my heart is with your heart*, then love me with a tender affection, as a friend that is *closer than one's nearest kin*.[4] Love me as a brother or sister in Christ, a fellow citizen of the New Jerusalem,[5] a fellow soldier engaged in the same warfare,[6] under the same captain of our salvation.[7] Love me as a companion in the kingdom and patient endurance of Jesus,[8] and a joint heir of his glory.[9]

Love me, in a higher degree than you do the bulk of humanity, with this kind of love: long-suffering and kind; patient when I am ignorant or act inappropriately; bearing my burden instead of increasing it; tender, soft, and compassionate; not envying, if at any time it pleases God to prosper me in his work even more than you.

Love me with the love that is not offended by my foolishness or weaknesses, or even when it seems to you that I act against the will of God.

Love me in such a way that you think no evil of me; put away all jealousy and suspicion.

Love me with the love that covers all things,[10] never revealing to others my faults or weaknesses; that believes all things,[11] being always willing to think the best of me, and give me the benefit of the doubt by taking all my words and actions in the best way possible; that hopes all things,[12] either that I never did whatever bad thing is said about me, or that I didn't do it the way you were told, or at least that I did it with good intentions, or I gave in to a sudden stress of temptation instead of doing it deliberately.

And hope to the end that whatever is wrong in me will, by the grace of God, be corrected, and whatever is missing in me will be supplied through the riches of God's mercy in Christ Jesus.

Pray for Me

I also mean a second thing.

Remember me to God in all your prayers. Wrestle with God on my behalf, that he would quickly correct anything he sees to be wrong in me, and supply what I am lacking. In your times of deepest prayer, when you sense that God is right there with you, beg him to make my heart more like your heart, more right both toward God and toward people. Ask him to give me a fuller conviction of things not seen,[13] and a stronger understanding of the love of God in Christ Jesus.[14] Pray that I may more steadily walk by faith, not by sight,[15] and may more earnestly grasp eternal life.[16]

Pray that the love of God and all humanity may be more and more poured into my heart. Pray that I may be more passionate and active in doing the will of my Father who is in heaven,[17] more zealous of good deeds,[18] and more careful to avoid any appearance of evil.[19]

Encourage Me

And I mean a third thing.

Provoke me to love and good deeds. [20]As you have opportunity, back up your prayers by speaking to me, in love,[21] whatever you believe I need to hear for my soul's health. Encourage me in the work God has given me to do, and instruct me in how to do it more perfectly.

Indeed, give me a friendly kick, and tell me about it,[22] whenever I seem to you to be doing my own will instead of the will of him who sent me.[23] Don't worry about offending me. Speak up and tell me whatever you believe will help me correct my faults, strengthen my weakness, build me up in love, or make me better fit in any way for the Master's use.

Help Me

I mean one more thing.

Love me not with your words only, but in truth and action.[24] As far as your conscience will let you, without giving up your own understandings and your own way of worshiping God, join with me in God's work, and let us go on hand in hand.

Certainly you can go this far: wherever you are, speak respectfully of God's work, no matter who God uses to do it, and speak kindly of God's messengers. And, as far as you can, don't just sympathize with them when they run into difficulty or distress, but help them out, cheerfully and effectively, so they may glorify God because of you.[25]

Not Just Me

Notice two things about what we have just said.

First, whatever love, whatever words or works of love, whatever spiritual or worldly assistance I claim from those whose heart is right as my heart is with theirs, I am ready, by the grace of God and as far as I am able, to give to them.

Second, I have not made this claim just for myself, but for everyone whose heart is right toward God and people, so we may all love one another as Christ has loved us.[26]

* * *

Discussion Questions

(1) Wesley is willing to take the hand of anyone whose heart is right. Thinking back to last week's discussion, summarize how he defines a right heart.

(2) "I can no more choose what I think than I can choose what I see or hear."

- Is Wesley saying it's impossible to change opinions?
- If not, what is he saying?

(3) How is Wesley's description of love different from the way our culture commonly defines it?

- Have you ever experienced this kind of love?
- Is this kind of love an emotion, a way of acting, or what?

- Based on Wesley's definition, how can you do a better job of loving your fellow Christians?

(4) Wesley gives a pretty detailed prayer request.

- How does his request compare with the usual prayer requests people share in church?
- How do your prayers for people compare with Wesley's request?

(5) The paraphrase says, "give me a friendly kick." Wesley's original words are, "smite me friendly."

- How willing are you to confront a fellow Christian if you think they are getting off track?
- How willing are you to have fellow Christians confront you?

* * *

Notes

[1] *"Can anyone withhold the water for baptizing these people who have received the Holy Spirit just as we have?"* (Acts 10:47)

[2] *And when he had given thanks, he broke it and said, "This is my body that is for you. Do this in remembrance of me." In the same way he took the cup also, after supper, saying, "This cup is the new covenant in my blood. Do this, as often as you drink it, in remembrance of me."* (1 Corinthians 11:24–25)

³ *But I say to you, love your enemies, bless those who curse you, do good to those who hate you, and pray for those who spitefully use you and persecute you,* (Matthew 5:44 NKJV)

⁴ *Some friends play at friendship but a true friend sticks closer than one's nearest kin.* (Proverbs 18:24)

⁵ *If you conquer, I will make you a pillar in the temple of my God; you will never go out of it. I will write on you the name of my God, and the name of the city of my God, the new Jerusalem that comes down from my God out of heaven, and my own new name.* (Revelation 3:12)

⁶ *For our struggle is not against enemies of blood and flesh, but against the rulers, against the authorities, against the cosmic powers of this present darkness, against the spiritual forces of evil in the heavenly places.* (Ephesians 6:12)

⁷ *For it was fitting for Him, for whom are all things and by whom are all things, in bringing many sons to glory, to make the captain of their salvation perfect through sufferings.* (Hebrews 2:10 NKJV)

⁸ *I, John, your brother who share with you in Jesus the persecution and the kingdom and the patient endurance, was on the island called Patmos because of the word of God and the testimony of Jesus.* (Revelation 1:9)

⁹ *And if children, then heirs, heirs of God and joint heirs with Christ—if, in fact, we suffer with him so that we may also be glorified with him.* (Romans 8:17)

¹⁰ *Above all, maintain constant love for one another, for love covers a multitude of sins.* (1 Peter 4:8)

¹¹ *It bears all things, believes all things, hopes all things, endures all things.* (1 Corinthians 13:7)

¹² *It bears all things, believes all things, hopes all things, endures all things.* (1 Corinthians 13:7)

¹³ *Now faith is the assurance of things hoped for, the conviction of things not seen.* (Hebrews 11:1)

¹⁴ *I pray that you may have the power to comprehend, with all the saints, what is the breadth and length and height and depth, and to know the love of Christ that surpasses knowledge, so that you may be filled with all the fullness of God.* (Ephesians 3:18–19)

¹⁵ *For we walk by faith, not by sight.* (2 Corinthians 5:7)

¹⁶ *Fight the good fight of the faith; take hold of the eternal life, to which you were called and for which you made the good confession in the presence of many witnesses.* (1 Timothy 6:12)

¹⁷ *Not everyone who says to me, "Lord, Lord," will enter the kingdom of heaven, but only the one who does the will of my Father in heaven.* (Matthew 7:21)

¹⁸ *He it is who gave himself for us that he might redeem us from all iniquity and purify for himself a people of his own who are zealous for good deeds.* (Titus 2:14)

¹⁹ *Abstain from every form of evil.* (1 Thessalonians 5:22) In the KJV, as in some modern translations, the word rendered "form" here is translated "appearance."

²⁰ *And let us consider how to provoke one another to love and good deeds.* (Hebrews 10:24)

²¹ *But speaking the truth in love, we must grow up in every way into him who is the head, into Christ.* (Ephesians 4:15)

²² *Let the righteous strike me; let the faithful correct me. Never let the oil of the wicked anoint my head, for my prayer is continually against their wicked deeds.* (Psalm 141:5)

²³ *Jesus said to them, "My food is to do the will of him who sent me and to complete his work."* (John 4:34)

²⁴ *Little children, let us love, not in word or speech, but in truth and action.* (1 John 3:18)

[25] *Through the testing of this ministry you glorify God by your obedience to the confession of the gospel of Christ and by the generosity of your sharing with them and with all others.* (2 Corinthians 9:13)

[26] *I give you a new commandment, that you love one another. Just as I have loved you, you also should love one another.* (John 13:34)

5

True Openness

Now when he departed from there, he met Jehonadab the son of Rechab, coming to meet him; and he greeted him and said to him, "Is your heart right, as my heart is toward your heart?" And Jehonadab answered, "It is." Jehu said, "If it is, give me your hand." — 2 Kings 10:15 NKJV

All of this brings us to the place where we can learn what it means to have a true spirit of openness. There is hardly any expression which has been more grossly misunderstood and more dangerously misapplied than this. But it will be easy for anyone who calmly considers the points made up to now to correct any such misunderstandings, and to prevent any such misapplication.

True Openness Does Not Accept Every Opinion

We learn, first, that true openness is not a speculative latitudi-narianism; in other words, it is not a philosophy that says all religions or religious opinions are equally true. This idea is the spawn of hell, not the offspring of heaven. This unsettledness of thought, this being *tossed to and fro and blown about by every wind of doctrine*,[1] is a great curse, not a blessing. It is an irreconcilable enemy, not a true friend, to real openness.

Those with a truly open spirit are not still trying to figure out their religion. They are as fixed as the sun in their judgment about the main branches of Christian doctrine. It is true that they are always ready to hear and consider whatever arguments are offered against their principles. But that openness doesn't show any wavering in their minds, and it doesn't cause any. They don't go limping between two opinions,[2] nor vainly try to blend them into one.

See this, you who don't know your own minds, you who call yourself open only because your understanding is muddy, because your mind is all in a mist, because you have no settled, consistent principles, but are for jumbling all opinions together; see and believe this: You have completely lost your way. You don't know where you are. You think you are being so Christlike, when in truth you are nearer the spirit of antichrist.[3] Go, first, and learn the basic elements of the gospel of Christ, and then you will learn what true openness is.

True Openness Does Not Accept Every Practice

The second thing we learn is that a truly open spirit is not any kind of practical latitudinarianism; that is, it doesn't claim that public worship is not important, or that how it is performed doesn't matter. This, likewise, would not be a blessing, but a curse. As long as this attitude exists, far from helping, it would be an unspeakable hindrance to the worshiping of God in spirit and in truth.[4]

But those of a truly open spirit, having weighed all the arguments, have no doubts or hesitations concerning the particular way of worship they join. They are clearly convinced that their manner of worshiping God is both scriptural and reasonable. They know of no other way that is more scriptural or more reasonable. Therefore, without wandering here and there, they stick close to their way of worshiping, and they praise God for the opportunity to do it.

True Openness Is Loyal

We learn a third thing: having an open spirit doesn't mean that you think it's not important what church you go to or which congregation you belong to. This is another kind of latitudinarianism, no less absurd and unscriptural than the first two. But truly open people are far from this kind of thinking.

They are loyal to their congregation as well as their principles. They are united to it, not only in spirit, but by all the outward ties of Christian fellowship. There they participate in all that God has commanded. There they receive the Lord's Supper. There they pour out their souls in public prayer, and join in public praise and thanksgiving. There they rejoice to hear the message of forgiveness, the good news of the grace of God.

On solemn occasions, they join there with their closest and best-loved sisters and brothers to seek God by fasting. They all watch over each other's souls in love, admonishing, exhorting, comforting, reproving, and in every way building up each other in the faith. They regard each other as family; and therefore, according to the ability God has given them, they naturally care for each other, and make sure each one has *everything needed for life and godliness.*[5]

True Openness Is Universal Love

But even though they are steadily fixed in their religious principles about what they believe to be the truth of Jesus; even though they firmly adhere to the kind of worship they judge to be most acceptable to God; and even though they are united by the tenderest and closest ties to one particular congregation — still, their hearts are open to every person, those they know and those they don't; they embrace with strong and cordial affection neighbors and strangers, friends and enemies.

This universal love is the sign of an open spirit, for love alone applies the label. Universal love is the spirit of openness. If, then, we take this word in the strictest sense, those of an open spirit are those who, in the ways described above, give their hand to all whose hearts are right with their hearts.

They know how to value, and praise God for, all the advantages they enjoy with regard to knowing the things of God, true scriptural worship, and, above all, their union with a congregation who fears God and works righteousness. They guard these blessings with the strictest care, as the apple of their eye.

At the same time, they love all Christians, no matter their religious opinions or worship style or congregation. They love everyone who believes in the Lord Jesus Christ, loves God and people, and seeks to please and not offend God by avoiding evil and being passionate for good works. They love them as friends, as sisters and brothers in the Lord, as members of Christ and children of God, as fellow participants now in the present kingdom of God, and fellow heirs of God's eternal kingdom.

Those who have a truly open spirit keep other Christians continually in their heart. They feel great tenderness toward them and long for their welfare. Because of this, they do not cease to remember all Christians before God in prayer, and defend them before people. Their words to all Christians are intended for comfort and strengthening of their souls in God. They help them as far as they can in all things, spiritual and material. They are ready to spend and be spent[6] for them; indeed, to lay down their lives for their sake.[7]

You, Christian!

You, Christian, think about these things! If you are already on this path, go on. If somehow you had mistaken the path, bless God who brought you back!

And now, run the race which is set before you,[8] in the royal way of universal love. Be careful not to be either wavering in your thoughts, or bound up in your emotions, but keep an even pace, rooted in the faith once entrusted to the saints,[9] and grounded in love, in true open love, until you are swallowed up in love for ever and ever!

* * *

51

Discussion Questions

(1) Wesley has harsh words for those who believe all religions or religious opinions or practices are equally true (the "latitudinarian" philosophy).

- Is he a bigot?
- Is it possible for all religions to be equally true, or do some make claims or have beliefs that completely contradict claims or beliefs of others?
- What kinds of things can be true for one person but not another, and what kinds of things are either true or not true in an absolute sense?

(2) Have you ever thought about whether the way your church worships is more scriptural and reasonable than others, or have you just accepted it without thinking about it too much?

(3) Wesley describes a feeling of family loyalty each Christian should feel for their own congregation.

- How much do you feel that way about your congregation? How do you show it?
- Do you know anyone who frequently changes churches? Are they being wise consumers of religion, or are they missing something?

(4) If an outsider looked at all the churches in your area, how much would they see a demonstration of universal love among them?

- What can your church do to improve that?

(5) Look back at this whole study.

- What was the best thing about it?
- Did it inspire you to do anything personally?
- Did it inspire you to encourage your church to do anything?
- Would you like to do another similar study?

(6) Extra credit: sing Charles Wesley's hymn, "Catholic Love" (Appendix 1), and notice how closely it follows this sermon. Use the tune of "Faith of Our Fathers."

* * *

Notes

[1] *We must no longer be children, tossed to and fro and blown about by every wind of doctrine, by people's trickery, by their craftiness in deceitful scheming.* (Ephesians 4:14)

[2] *Elijah then came near to all the people, and said, "How long will you go limping with two different opinions? If the Lord is God, follow him; but if Baal, then follow him." The people did not answer him a word.* (1 Kings 18:21)

[3] *And every spirit that does not confess Jesus is not from God. And this is the spirit of the antichrist, of which you have heard that it is coming; and now it is already in the world.* (1 John 4:3)

[4] *God is spirit, and those who worship him must worship in spirit and truth.* (John 4:24)

⁵ *His divine power has given us everything needed for life and godliness, through the knowledge of him who called us by his own glory and goodness.* (2 Peter 1:3)

⁶ *I will most gladly spend and be spent for you. If I love you more, am I to be loved less?* (2 Corinthians 12:15)

⁷ *No one has greater love than this, to lay down one's life for one's friends.* (John 15:13)

⁸ *Therefore, since we are surrounded by so great a cloud of witnesses, let us also lay aside every weight and the sin that clings so closely, and let us run with perseverance the race that is set before us.* (Hebrews 12:1)

⁹ *Beloved, while eagerly preparing to write to you about the salvation we share, I find it necessary to write and appeal to you to contend for the faith that was once for all entrusted to the saints.* (Jude 3)

Appendix 1: Sermon in Song

John Wesley's brother, Charles Wesley, wrote over 3,000 hymns in his lifetime. Many of them put the essence of John's teaching to rhyme and music. This hymn, "Catholic Love," is a great example. It was added at the end of this sermon in some of the early printed editions. You can sing it to the tune of "Faith of Our Fathers."

As with the title of John's sermon, the word "catholic" is used here in its old English sense of universal or open-minded. (See the Introduction.)

Weary of all this wordy strife,
   These notions, forms, and modes, and names,
   To Thee, the Way, the Truth, the Life,
   Whose love my simple heart inflames,
   Divinely taught, at last I fly,
   With Thee and Thine to live and die.

Forth from the midst of Babel brought,
   Parties and sects I cast behind;
   Enlarged my heart, and free my thought,
   Where'er the latent truth I find
   The latent truth with joy to own,
   And bow to Jesus' name alone.

Redeem'd by Thine almighty grace,
   I taste my glorious liberty,
   With open arms the world embrace,
   But cleave to those who cleave to Thee;
   But only in Thy saints delight,
   Who walk with God in purest white.

One with the little flock I rest,
   The members sound who hold the head.
   The chosen few, with pardon blest
   And by th' anointing Spirit led
   Into the mind that was in Thee
   Into the depths of Deity.

My brethren, friends, and kinsmen these
   Who do my heavenly Father's will;
   Who aim at perfect holiness,
   And all Thy counsels to fulfil,
   Athirst to be whate'er Thou art,
   And love their God with all their heart.

For these, howe'er in flesh disjoin'd,
   Where'er dispersed o'er earth abroad,
   Unfeign'd, unbounded love I find
   And constant as the life of God
   Fountain of life, from thence it sprung,
   As pure, as even, and as strong.

Join'd to the hidden church unknown
   In this sure bond of perfectness
   Obscurely safe, I dwell alone

And glory in th' uniting grace,
To me, to each believer given,
To all Thy saints in earth and heaven.

Appendix 2: John Wesley's Original Words

Catholic Spirit

By John Wesley

Sermon #39, first published in 1750. This version is from The Works of John Wesley, *Third American Edition, 1872, edited by Thomas Jackson.*

> "And when he was departed thence, he lighted on Je-
> honadab the son of Rechab coming to meet him, and he
> saluted him, and said to him, Is thine heart right, as my
> heart is with thy heart? And Jehonadab answered: It is. If
> it be, give me thine hand." 2 Kings 10:15.

1. It is allowed even by those who do not pay this great debt, that love is due to all mankind, the royal law, "Thou shalt love thy neighbor as thyself," carrying its own evidence to all that hear it: and that, not according to the miserable construction put upon it by the zealots of old times, "Thou shalt love thy neighbor," thy relation, acquaintance, friend, "and hate thine enemy;" not so; "I say unto you," said

our Lord, "Love your enemies, bless them that curse you, do good to them that hate you, and pray for them that despitefully use you, and persecute you; that ye may be the children," may appear so to all mankind, "of your Father which is in heaven; who maketh his sun to rise on the evil and on the good, and sendeth rain on the just and on the unjust."

2. But it is sure, there is a peculiar love which we owe to those that love God. So David: "All my delight is upon the saints that are in the earth, and upon such as excel in virtue." And so a greater than he: "A new commandment I give unto you, That ye love one another: as I have loved you, that ye also love one another. By this shall all men know that ye are My disciples, if ye have love one to another" (John 13:34, 35). This is that love on which the Apostle John so frequently and strongly insists: "This," saith he, "is the message that ye heard from the beginning, that we should love one another" (1 John 3:11). "Hereby perceive we the love of God, because he laid down his life for us: and we ought," if love should call us thereto, "to lay down our lives for the brethren" (verse 16). And again: "Beloved, let us love one another: for love is of God. He that loveth not, knoweth not God; for God is love" (4:7, 8). "Not that we loved God, but that he loved us, and sent his Son to be the propitiation for our sins. Beloved, if God so loved us, we ought also to love one another" (verses 10, 11).

3. All men approve of this; but do all men practise it? Daily experience shows the contrary. Where are even the Christians who "love one another as he hath given us commandment?" How many hindrances lie in the way! The two grand, general hindrances are, first, that they

cannot all think alike and, in consequence of this, secondly, they cannot all walk alike; but in several smaller points their practice must differ in proportion to the difference of their sentiments.

4. But although a difference in opinions or modes of worship may prevent an entire external union, yet need it prevent our union in affection? Though we cannot think alike, may we not love alike? May we not be of one heart, though we are not of one opinion? Without all doubt, we may. Herein all the children of God may unite, nevertheless these smaller differences. These remaining as they are, they may forward one another in love and in good works.

5. Surely in this respect the example of Jehu himself, as mixed a character as he was of, is well worthy both the attention and imitation of every serious Christian. "And when he was departed thence, he lighted on Jehonadab the son of Rechab coming to meet him; and he saluted him, and said to him, Is thine heart right, as my heart is with thy heart? And Jehonadab answered, It is. If it be, give me thine hand."

The text naturally divides itself into two parts: —First, a question proposed by Jehu to Jehonadab: "Is thine heart right, as my heart is with thy heart?" Secondly, an offer made on Jehonadab's answering, "It is: "If it be, give me thine hand."

I.

1. And, first, let us consider the question proposed by Jehu to Jehonadab, "Is thine heart right, as my heart is with thy heart?"

The very first thing we may observe in these words, is, that here is no inquiry concerning Jehonadab's opinions. And yet it is certain, he held some which were very uncommon, indeed quite peculiar to himself; and some which had a close influence upon his practice; on which, likewise, he laid so great a stress, as to entail them upon his children's children, to their latest posterity. This is evident from the account given by Jeremiah many years after his death: "I took Jaazaniah and his brethren and all his sons, and the whole house of the Rechabites, . . . and set before them pots full of wine, and cups, and said unto them, Drink ye wine. But they said, We will drink no wine: for Jonadab," or Jehonadab, "the son of Rechab, our father" (it would be less ambiguous, if the words were placed thus: "Jehonadab our father, the son of Rechab," out of love and reverence to whom, he probably desired his descendants might be called by his name), "commanded us, saying, ye shall drink no wine, neither ye, nor your sons for ever. Neither shall ye build house, nor sow seed; nor plant vineyard, nor have any: but all your days ye shall dwell in tents.... And we have obeyed, and done according to all that Jonadab our father commanded us" (Jer. 35:3-10).

2. And yet Jehu (although it seems to have been his manner both in things secular and religious, to drive furiously) does not concern himself at all with any of these things, but lets Jehonadab abound in his own sense. And neither of them appears to have given the other the least disturbance touching the opinions which he maintained.

3. It is very possible, that many good men now also may entertain peculiar opinions; and some of them may be as singular herein as even Jehonadab was. And it is certain, so long as we know but in part, that all men will not see all things alike. It is an unavoidable consequence of the present weakness and shortness of human understanding, that several men will be of several minds in religion as well as in common life. So it has been from the beginning of the world, and so it will be "till

the restitution of all things."

4. Nay, farther: although every man necessarily believes that every particular opinion which he holds is true (for to believe any opinion is not true, is the same thing as not to hold it); yet can no man be assured that all his own opinions, taken together, are true. Nay, every thinking man is assured they are not, seeing _humanum est errare et nescire_: "To be ignorant of many things, and to mistake in some, is the necessary condition of humanity." This, therefore, he is sensible, is his own case. He knows, in the general, that he himself is mistaken; although in what particulars he mistakes, he does not, perhaps he cannot, know.

5. I say "perhaps he cannot know;" for who can tell how far invincible ignorance may extend? or (that comes to the same thing) invincible prejudice? —which is often so fixed in tender minds, that it is afterwards impossible to tear up what has taken so deep a root. And who can say, unless he knew every circumstance attending it, how far any mistake is culpable? seeing all guilt must suppose some concurrence of the will; of which he only can judge who searcheth the heart.

6. Every wise man, therefore, will allow others the same liberty of thinking which he desires they should allow him; and will no more insist on their embracing his opinions, than he would have them to insist on his embracing theirs. He bears with those who differ from him, and only asks him with whom he desires to unite in love that single question, "Is thy heart right, as my heart is with thy heart?"

7. We may, secondly, observe, that here is no inquiry made concerning Jehonadab's mode of worship; although it is highly probable there was, in this respect also, a very wide difference between them. For we may well believe Jehonadab, as well

as all his posterity, worshipped God at Jerusalem! whereas Jehu did not: he had more regard to state-policy than religion. And, therefore, although he slew the worshippers of Baal, and "destroyed Baal out of Israel," yet from the convenient sin of Jeroboam, the worship of the "golden calves," he "departed not" (2 Kings 10:29).

8. But even among men of an upright heart, men who desire to "have a conscience void of offence," it must needs be, that, as long as there are various opinions, there will be various ways of worshipping God; seeing a variety of opinion necessarily implies a variety of practice. And as, in all ages, men have differed in nothing more than in their opinions concerning the Supreme Being, so in nothing have they more differed from each other, than in the manner of worshipping him. Had this been only in the heathen world, it would not have been at all surprising: for we know, these "by" their "wisdom knew not God;" nor, therefore, could they know how to worship him. But is it not strange, that even in the Christian world, although they all agree in the general, "God is a Spirit; and they that worship him must worship him in spirit and in truth;" yet the particular modes of worshipping God are almost as various as among the heathens?

9. And how shall we choose among so much variety? No man can choose for, or prescribe to, another. But every one must follow the dictates of his own conscience, in simplicity and godly sincerity. He must be fully persuaded in his own mind and then act according to the best light he has. Nor has any creature power to constrain another to walk by his own rule. God has given no right to any of the children of men thus to lord it over the conscience of his brethren; but every man must judge for himself, as every man must give an account of

himself to God.

10. Although, therefore, every follower of Christ is obliged, by the very nature of the Christian institution, to be a member of some particular congregation or other, some Church, as it is usually termed (which implies a particular manner of worshipping God; for "two cannot walk together unless they be agreed"); yet none can be obliged by any power on earth but that of his own conscience, to prefer this or that congregation to another, this or that particular manner of worship. I know it is commonly supposed, that the place of our birth fixes the Church to which we ought to belong; that one, for instance, who is born in England, ought to be a member of that which is styled the Church of England, and consequently, to worship God in the particular manner which is prescribed by that Church. I was once a zealous maintainer of this; but I find many reasons to abate of this zeal. I fear it is attended with such difficulties as no reasonable man can get over. Not the least of which is, that if this rule had took place, there could have been no Reformation from Popery; seeing it entirely destroys the right of private judgement, on which that whole Reformation stands.

11. I dare not, therefore, presume to impose my mode of worship on any other. I believe it is truly primitive and apostolical: but my belief is no rule for another. I ask not, therefore, of him with whom I would unite in love, Are you of my church, of my congregation? Do you receive the same form of church government, and allow the same church officers, with me? Do you join in the same form of prayer wherein I worship God? I inquire not, Do you receive the supper of the Lord in the same posture and manner that I do? nor whether, in the administration of baptism, you agree with me in admitting sureties for the baptized, in the manner of administering it;

or the age of those to whom it should be administered. Nay, I ask not of you (as clear as I am in my own mind), whether you allow baptism and the Lord's supper at all. Let all these things stand by: we will talk of them, if need be, at a more convenient season, my only question at present is this, "Is thine heart right, as my heart is with thy heart?"

12. But what is properly implied in the question? I do not mean, What did Jehu imply therein? But, What should a follower of Christ understand thereby, when he proposes it to any of his brethren?

The first thing implied is this: Is thy heart right with God? Dost thou believe his being and his perfections? his eternity, immensity, wisdom, power? his justice, mercy, and truth? Dost thou believe that he now "upholdeth all things by the word of his power?" and that he governs even the most minute, even the most noxious, to his own glory, and the good of them that love him? hast thou a divine evidence, a supernatural conviction, of the things of God? Dost thou "walk by faith not by sight?" looking not at temporal things, but things eternal?

13. Dost thou believe in the Lord Jesus Christ, "God over all, blessed for ever?" Is he revealed in thy soul? Dost thou know Jesus Christ and him crucified? Does he dwell in thee, and thou in him? Is he formed in thy heart by faith? having absolutely disclaimed all thy own works, thy own righteousness, hast thou "submitted thyself unto the righteousness of God, which is by faith in Christ Jesus? Art thou "found in him, not having thy own righteousness, but the righteousness which is by faith?" And art thou, through him, "fighting the good fight of faith, and laying hold of eternal life?"

14. Is thy faith _energoumenE di' agapEs_, —filled with the energy of love? Dost thou love God (I do not say "above

all things," for it is both an unscriptural and an ambiguous expression, but) "with all thy heart, and with all thy mind, and with all thy soul, and with all thy strength?" Dost thou seek all thy happiness in him alone? And dost thou find what thou seekest? Does thy soul continually "magnify the Lord, and thy spirit rejoice in God thy Savior?" Having learned "in everything to give thanks, dost thou find "it is a joyful and a pleasant thing to be thankful?" Is God the center of thy soul, the sum of all thy desires? Art thou accordingly laying up thy treasure in heaven, and counting all things else dung and dross? Hath the love of God cast the love of the world out of thy soul? Then thou art "crucified to the world;" thou art dead to all below; and thy "life is hid with Christ in God."

15. Art thou employed in doing, "not thy own will, but the will of him that sent thee" —of him that sent thee down to sojourn here awhile, to spend a few days in a strange land, till, having finished the work he hath given thee to do, thou return to thy Father's house? Is it thy meat and drink "to do the will of thy Father which is in heaven?" Is thine eye single in all things? always fixed on him? always looking unto Jesus? Dost thou point at him in whatever thou doest? in all thy labor, thy business, thy conversation? aiming only at the glory of God in all, "whatever thou doest, either in word or deed, doing it all in the name of the Lord Jesus; giving thanks unto God, even the Father, through him?"

16. Does the love of God constrain thee to serve him with fear, to "rejoice unto him with reverence?" Art thou more afraid of displeasing God, than either of death or hell? Is nothing so terrible to thee as the thought of offending the eyes of his glory? Upon this ground, dost thou "hate all evil ways," every transgression of his holy and perfect law; and herein "exercise

thyself, to have a conscience void of offence toward God, and toward man?"

17. Is thy heart right toward thy neighbor? Dost thou love as thyself, all mankind, without exception? "If you love those only that love you, what thank have ye?" Do you "love your enemies?" Is your soul full of good-will, of tender affection, toward them? Do you love even the enemies of God, the unthankful and unholy? Do your bowels yearn over them? Could you "wish yourself" temporally "accursed" for their sake? And do you show this by "blessing them that curse you, and praying for those that despitefully use you, and persecute you?"

18. Do you show your love by your works? While you have time as you have opportunity, do you in fact "do good to all men," neighbors or strangers, friends or enemies, good or bad? Do you do them all the good you can; endeavoring to supply all their wants; assisting them both in body and soul, to the uttermost of your power? —If thou art thus minded, may every Christian say, yea, if thou art but sincerely desirous of it, and following on till thou attain, then "thy heart is right, as my heart is with thy heart."

II.

1."If it be, give me thy hand." I do not mean, "Be of my opinion." You need not: I do not expect or desire it. Neither do I mean, "I will be of your opinion." I cannot, it does not depend on my choice: I can no more think, than I can see or hear, as I will. Keep you your opinion; I mine; and that as steadily as ever. You need not even endeavor to come over to me, or bring me over to you. I do not desire you to dispute those points, or to hear or speak one word concerning them. Let all opinions alone on one side and the other: only "give me thine hand."

2.I do not mean, "Embrace my modes of worship," or, "I

will embrace yours." This also is a thing which does not depend either on your choice or mine. We must both act as each is fully persuaded in his own mind. Hold you fast that which you believe is most acceptable to God, and I will do the same. I believe the Episcopal form of church government to be scriptural and apostolical. If you think the Presbyterian or Independent is better, think so still, and act accordingly. I believe infants ought to be baptized; and that this may be done either by dipping or sprinkling. If you are otherwise persuaded, be so still, and follow your own persuasion. It appears to me, that forms of prayer are of excellent use, particularly in the great congregation. If you judge extemporary prayer to be of more use, act suitable to your own judgement. My sentiment is, that I ought not to forbid water, wherein persons may be baptized; and that I ought to eat bread and drink wine, as a memorial of my dying Master: however, if you are not convinced of this act according to the light you have. I have no desire to dispute with you one moment upon any of the preceding heads. Let all these smaller points stand aside. Let them never come into sight "If thine heart is as my heart," if thou lovest God and all mankind, I ask no more: "give me thine hand."

3. I mean, first, love me: and that not only as thou lovest all mankind; not only as thou lovest thine enemies, or the enemies of God, those that hate thee, that "despitefully use thee, and persecute thee;" not only as a stranger, as one of whom thou knowest neither good nor evil, —I am not satisfied with this, —no; "if thine heart be right, as mine with thy heart," then love me with a very tender affection, as a friend that is closer than a brother; as a brother in Christ, a fellow citizen of the New Jerusalem, a fellow soldier engaged in the same warfare, under the same Captain of our salvation. Love me as a companion in

the kingdom and patience of Jesus, and a joint heir of his glory.

4.Love me (but in a higher degree than thou dost the bulk of mankind) with the love that is long-suffering and kind; that is patient, —if I am ignorant or out of the way, bearing and not increasing my burden; and is tender, soft, and compassionate still; that envieth not, if at any time it please God to prosper me in his work even more than thee. Love me with the love that is not provoked, either at my follies or infirmities; or even at my acting (if it should sometimes so appear to thee) not according to the will of God. Love me so as to think no evil of me; to put away all jealousy and evil-surmising. Love me with the love that covereth all things; that never reveals either my faults or infirmities, —that believeth all things; is always willing to think the best, to put the fairest construction on all my words and actions, —that hopeth all things; either that the thing related was never done; or not done with such circumstances as are related; or, at least, that it was done with a good-intention, or in a sudden stress of temptation. And hope to the end, that whatever is amiss will, by the grace of God, be corrected; and whatever is wanting, supplied, through the riches of his mercy in Christ Jesus.

5. I mean, Secondly, commend me to God in all thy prayers; wrestle with him in my behalf, that he would speedily correct what he sees amiss, and supply what is wanting in me. In thy nearest access to the throne of grace, beg of him who is then very present with thee, that my heart may be more as thy heart, more right both toward God and toward man; that I may have a fuller conviction of things not seen, and a stronger view of the love of God in Christ Jesus; may more steadily walk by faith, not by sight; and more earnestly grasp eternal life. Pray that the love of God and of all mankind may be more largely poured

into my heart; that I may be more fervent and active in doing the will of my Father which is in heaven, more zealous of good works, and more careful to abstain from all appearance of evil.

6. I mean, Thirdly, provoke me to love and to good works. Second thy prayer, as thou hast opportunity, by speaking to me, in love, whatever thou believest to be for my soul's health. Quicken me in the work which God has given me to do, and instruct me how to do it more perfectly. Yea, "smite me friendly, and reprove me," whereinsoever I appear to thee to be doing rather my own will, than the will of him that sent me. O speak and spare not, whatever thou believest may conduce, either to the amending my faults, the strengthening my weakness, the building me up in love, or the making me more fit, in any kind, for the Master's use.

7. I mean, Lastly, love me not in word only, but in deed and in truth. So far as in conscience thou canst (retaining still thy own opinions, and thy own manner of worshipping God), join with me in the work of God; and let us go on hand in hand. And thus far, it is certain, thou mayest go. Speak honorably wherever thou art, of the work of God, by whomsoever he works, and kindly of his messengers. And, if it be in thy power, not only sympathize with them when they are in any difficulty or distress, but give them a cheerful and effectual assistance, that they may glorify God on thy behalf.

8. Two things should be observed with regard to what has been spoken under this last head: the one, that whatever love, whatever offices of love, whatever spiritual or temporal assistance, I claim from him whose heart is right, as my heart is with his, the same I am ready, by the grace of God, according to my measure, to give him: the other, that I have not made this claim in behalf of myself only, but of all whose heart is

right toward God and man, that we may all love one another as Christ hath loved us.

III.

1. One inference we may make from what has been said. We may learn from hence, what is a catholic spirit.

There is scarce any expression which has been more grossly misunderstood, and more dangerously misapplied, than this: but it will be easy for any who calmly consider the preceding observations, to correct any such misapprehensions of it, and to prevent any such misapplication.

For, from hence we may learn, first, that a catholic spirit is not speculative latitudinarianism. It is not an indifference to all opinions: this is the spawn of hell, not the offspring of heaven. This unsettledness of thought, this being "driven to and fro, and tossed about with every wind of doctrine," is a great curse, not a blessing, an irreconcilable enemy, not a friend, to true catholicism. A man of a truly catholic spirit has not now his religion to seek. He is fixed as the sun in his judgement concerning the main branches of Christian doctrine. It is true, he is always ready to hear and weigh whatever can be offered against his principles; but as this does not show any wavering in his own mind, so neither does it occasion any. He does not halt between two opinions, nor vainly endeavor to blend them into one. Observe this, you who know not what spirit ye are of: who call yourselves men of a catholic spirit, only because you are of a muddy understanding; because your mind is all in a mist; because you have no settled, consistent principles, but are for jumbling all opinions together. Be convinced, that you have quite missed your way; you know not where you are. You think you are got into the very spirit of Christ; when, in truth, you are nearer the spirit of Antichrist. Go, first, and learn the first elements of the gospel of Christ, and then shall you learn to be of a truly catholic spirit.

2. From what has been said, we may learn, secondly, that a catholic spirit is not any kind of practical latitudinarianism. It is not indifference as to public worship, or as to the outward manner of performing it. This, likewise, would not be a blessing but a curse. Far from being an help thereto, it would, so long as it remained, be an unspeakable hindrance to the worshipping of God in spirit and in truth. But the man of a truly catholic spirit, having weighed all things in the balance of the sanctuary, has no doubt, no scruple at all, concerning that particular mode of worship wherein he joins. He is clearly convinced, that this manner of worshipping God is both scriptural and rational. He knows none in the world which is more scriptural, none which is more rational. Therefore, without rambling hither and thither, he cleaves close thereto, and praises God for the opportunity of so doing.

3. Hence we may, thirdly, learn, that a catholic spirit is not indifference to all congregations. This is another sort of latitudinarianism, no less absurd and unscriptural than the former. But it is far from a man of a truly catholic spirit. He is fixed in his congregation as well as his principles. He is united to one, not only in spirit, but by all the outward ties of Christian fellowship. There he partakes of all the ordinances of God. There he receives the supper of the Lord. There he pours out his soul in public prayer, and joins in public praise and thanksgiving. There he rejoices to hear the word of reconciliation, the gospel of the grace of God. With these his nearest, his best-beloved brethren, on solemn occasions, he seeks God by fasting. These particularly he watches over in love, as they do over his soul; admonishing, exhorting,

comforting, reproving, and every way building up each other in the faith. These he regards as his own household; and therefore, according to the ability God has given him, naturally cares for them, and provides that they may have all the things that are needful for life and godliness.

4. But while he is steadily fixed in his religious principles in what he believes to be the truth as it is in Jesus; while he firmly adheres to that worship of God which he judges to be most acceptable in his sight; and while he is united by the tenderest and closest ties to one particular congregation, — his heart is enlarged toward all mankind, those he knows and those he does not; he embraces with strong and cordial affection neighbors and strangers, friends and enemies. This is catholic or universal love. And he that has this is of a catholic spirit. For love alone gives the title to this character: catholic love is a catholic spirit.

5. If, then, we take this word in the strictest sense, a man of a catholic spirit is one who, in the manner above-mentioned, gives his hand to all whose hearts are right with his heart: one who knows how to value, and praise God for, all the advantages he enjoys, with regard to the knowledge of the things of God, the true scriptural manner of worshipping him, and, above all, his union with a congregation fearing God and working righteousness: one who, retaining these blessings with the strictest care, keeping them as the apple of his eye, at the same time loves—as friends, as brethren in the Lord, as members of Christ and children of God, as joint partakers now of the present kingdom of God, and fellow heirs of his eternal kingdom—all, of whatever opinion or worship, or congregation, who believe in the Lord Jesus Christ; who love God and man; who, rejoicing to please, and fearing to offend God, are careful to abstain from evil, and zealous of good works. He is the man of a truly

catholic spirit, who bears all these continually upon his heart; who having an unspeakable tenderness for their persons, and longing for their welfare, does not cease to commend them to God in prayer, as well as to plead their cause before men; who speaks comfortably to them, and labors, by all his words, to strengthen their hands in God. He assists them to the uttermost of his power in all things, spiritual and temporal. He is ready "to spend and be spent for them;" yea, to lay down his life for their sake.

6. Thou, O man of God, think on these things! If thou art already in this way, go on. If thou hast heretofore mistook the path, bless God who hath brought thee back! And now run the race which is set before thee, in the royal way of universal love. Take heed, lest thou be either wavering in thy judgement, or straitened in thy bowels: but keep an even pace, rooted in the faith once delivered to the saints, and grounded in love, in true catholic love, till thou art swallowed up in love for ever and ever!

About the Author

Best known internationally as author of *Pastoring: The Nuts and Bolts*, in print in eight languages, David Wentz has a passion for helping people connect with God and make a difference. Combining 38 years as a pastor with a first career in engineering and graduate degrees from three very different seminaries (charismatic, mainstream, and Wesleyan-evangelical), he expresses God's truth in ways everyone can appreciate.

Raised in the Episcopal church, Dr. Wentz has also been part of Nazarene, Pentecostal Holiness, and non-denominational congregations. As a Methodist pastor he served small, large, and multicultural churches in rural, small-town, suburban, and urban settings, served as a regional church consultant in the Maryland – D.C. area, and led workshops for pastors internationally. In 2015 he retired to the rural Ozarks, where he writes, works in God's great outdoors, and oversees Doing

Christianity, Inc., a small non-profit devoted to equipping pastors in developing and minority-Christian countries.

In 1974, David married his college sweetheart, Paula. They have five children with wonderful spouses, and fourteen grandchildren.

The book of Ezekiel describes David's calling. Twenty-five hundred years ago God called Ezekiel to teach God's ways and proclaim the Holy Spirit, who revives dry bones and forms them into a dwelling for God and a source of living water that heals nations.

Bones are still dry today. God still wants to dwell among his people. Nations still need healing. And people still need to be taught God's ways and be moved by God's Spirit. That's what David calls "Doing Christianity."

You can connect with me on:

◑ https://www.pastordavidwentz.com

◧ https://www.facebook.com/profile.php?id=100064901162331

Also by David Wentz

Christianity is about more than just going to heaven when you die. It's about becoming like Jesus and living the Kingdom of God in this life. That not only blesses us, it blesses everyone around. That's what I call doing Christianity, and it's what my books are all about.

John Wesley's "The Character of a Methodist:" Set in Modern Language with Introduction and Suggestions for Group Use
A perennial best-seller since its publication, this summary of the root emphases of Wesley's teaching is required reading in today's turbulent times. Father of Methodism and grandfather of Pentecostalism and the Salvation Army, Wesley shows the character of a true Christian of any denomination. Part of the John Wesley in Modern Language series.

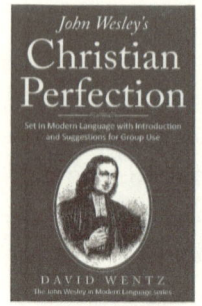

John Wesley's "Christian Perfection:" Set in Modern Language with Introduction and Suggestions for Group Use

"Christians aren't perfect, just forgiven." John Wesley doesn't agree. Christians not only can become perfect in this life — God commands us to!

Seeking perfection was an integral part of the explosive growth of Methodism for 100 years, even as it led to the persecution of those who practiced it. It's time to recover that power. Part of the John Wesley in Modern Language series.

"This book thrilled my soul and reinvigorated my hope." — Amazon reviewer

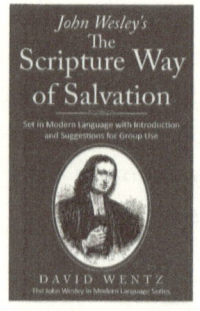

John Wesley's "The Scripture Way of Salvation:" Set in Modern Language with Introduction and Suggestions for Group Use

There's more to salvation than punching your ticket for heaven. John Wesley taught that full salvation means becoming completely holy in heart and life. This focus on personal holiness was at the heart of the Wesleyan revival. The many Methodist and Wesleyan denominations, the Pentecostal and holiness movements, and the Salvation Army all trace their lineage back to these teachings. Part of the John Wesley in Modern Language series.

John Wesley's "The New Birth:" Set in Modern Language with Introduction and Suggestions for Group Use

Is being good the way to heaven? Being religious? Jesus said, "You must be born again. John Wesley explains Jesus' words in this brief classic. One of the standard sermons Wesley required his circuit riders to learn and re-preach, *The New Birth* shows that religion and morality are good but new life in Jesus is vital. Part of the John Wesley in Modern Language series.

When Church Stops Working: Meeting With God in Your Living Room

For those who feel done with the institutional church, but still love Jesus. If you ever led a meeting or taught a class, you and your friends can be a fully functioning part of God's work in the world.

For pastors, here's a proven way to extend your reach by mentoring living-room church leaders and networks.

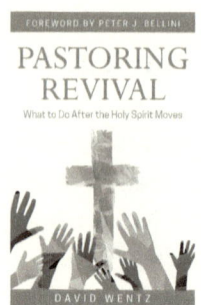

Pastoring Revival: What to Do After the Holy Spirit Moves

"Come, Holy Spirit!" Then what? Few pastors are trained what to do if God answers with unusual power. Drawing on two fascinating case studies, academic research, and his own thirty-eight years as a pastor, seeker, and student of revival, Dr. Wentz has produced a practical, engaging, Biblical, actionable guide to prepare every pastor for the next great move of God.

"It's hard to put to words how excited this book makes me. I have pastored for years . . . Read this book, and get ready." — Amazon reviewer

Pastoring: The Nuts and Bolts — Options and Best Practices for Leading a Church

Crossing denominations and cultures and solidly grounded in Scripture, *Pastoring* offers options and best practices instead of dogmatic assertions. It moves from God's purpose for the church to the pastor's personal life, then covers worship, preaching, leadership, administration. Includes issues relevant to charismatic and Pentecostal churches not often addressed. In eight languages and counting, *Pastoring* has blessed thousands of new and seasoned pastors. Study guide available to create a personalized action plan.

SCAN ME

Amazon Author Page

My Amazon Author Page has updated information and quick links to all my books.

If you're reading this in a physical book, connect your smartphone to the internet and focus the camera on the pattern to the left. Click on the button that appears on your screen and it should take you there!